Our Class Is Going GREEN!

Written and Illustrated by Mrs. Nickels' Kindergarten Class
At Oak Park Elementary in Bartlesville, Oklahoma

This book is dedicated to all the
"green" individuals
who realize the importance
of taking care of the environment.

Our story was created during our theme about the environment, and we were learning how

we should take care of our resources and our Earth. We all became excited about how we

could make a difference in our own school. After much discussion and learning,

we decided to put our ideas in a book. Then, during art class, we illustrated our book.

Our book was created by using materials from the recycling bin, which included

watercolor paintings, newspapers, and various paper scraps.

No! Not the color GREEN! Our class is learning how to be kind to the Earth.

To make our environment a better place,

here are some ways we are going GREEN.

Reduce

Reuse

Recycle

7

Walk to school...

INSTEAD of riding in cars.

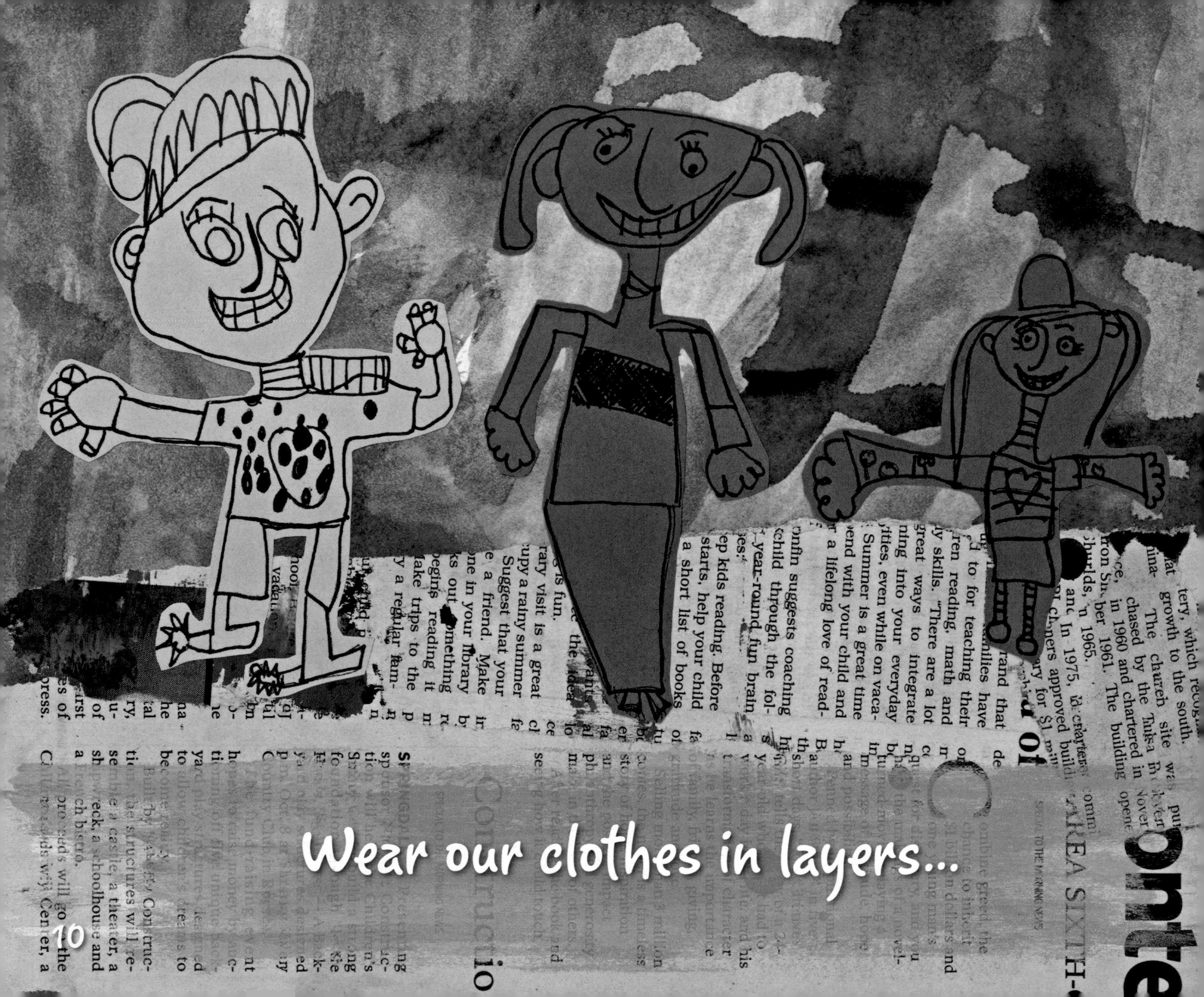

Wear our clothes in layers...

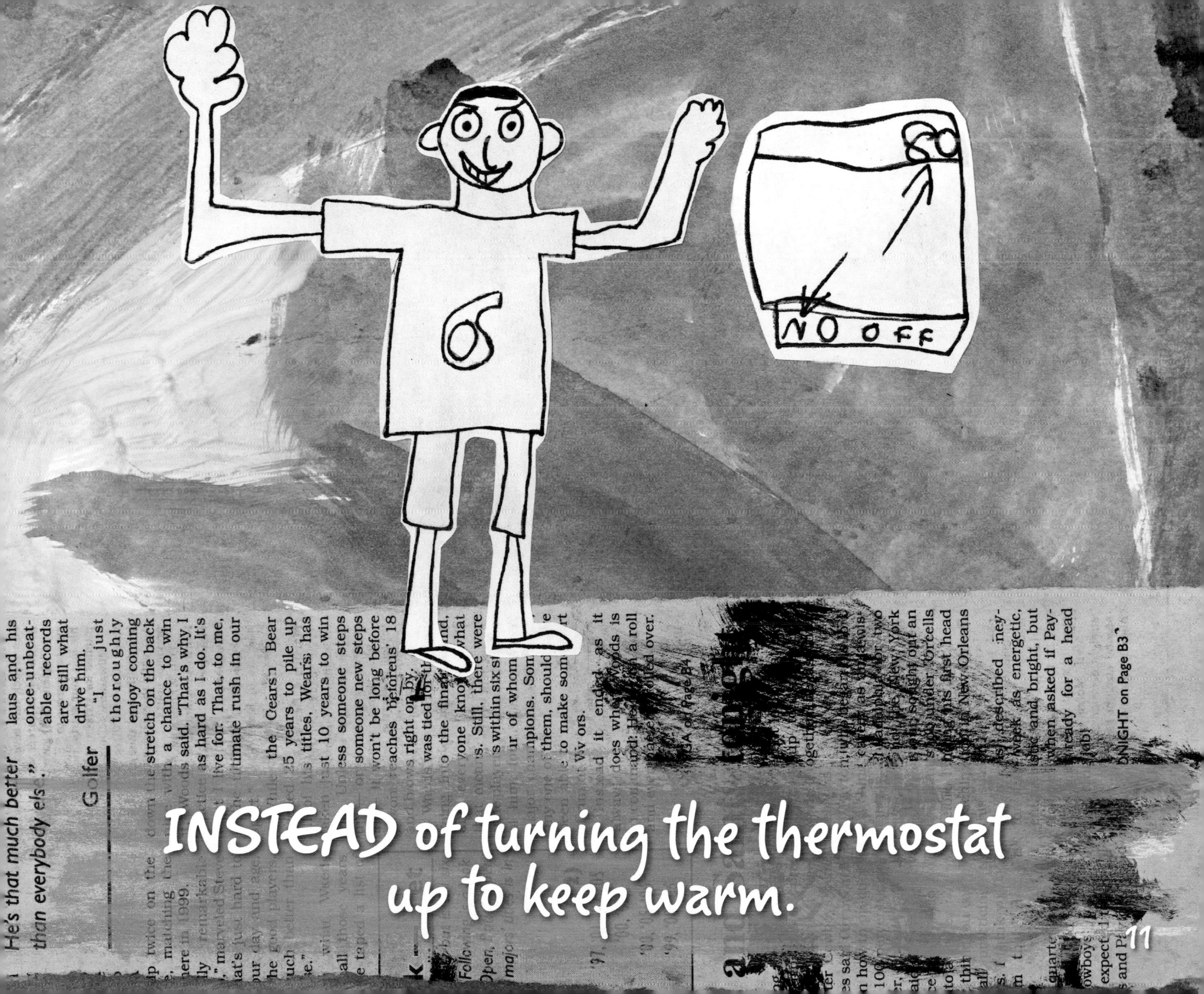

INSTEAD of turning the thermostat up to keep warm.

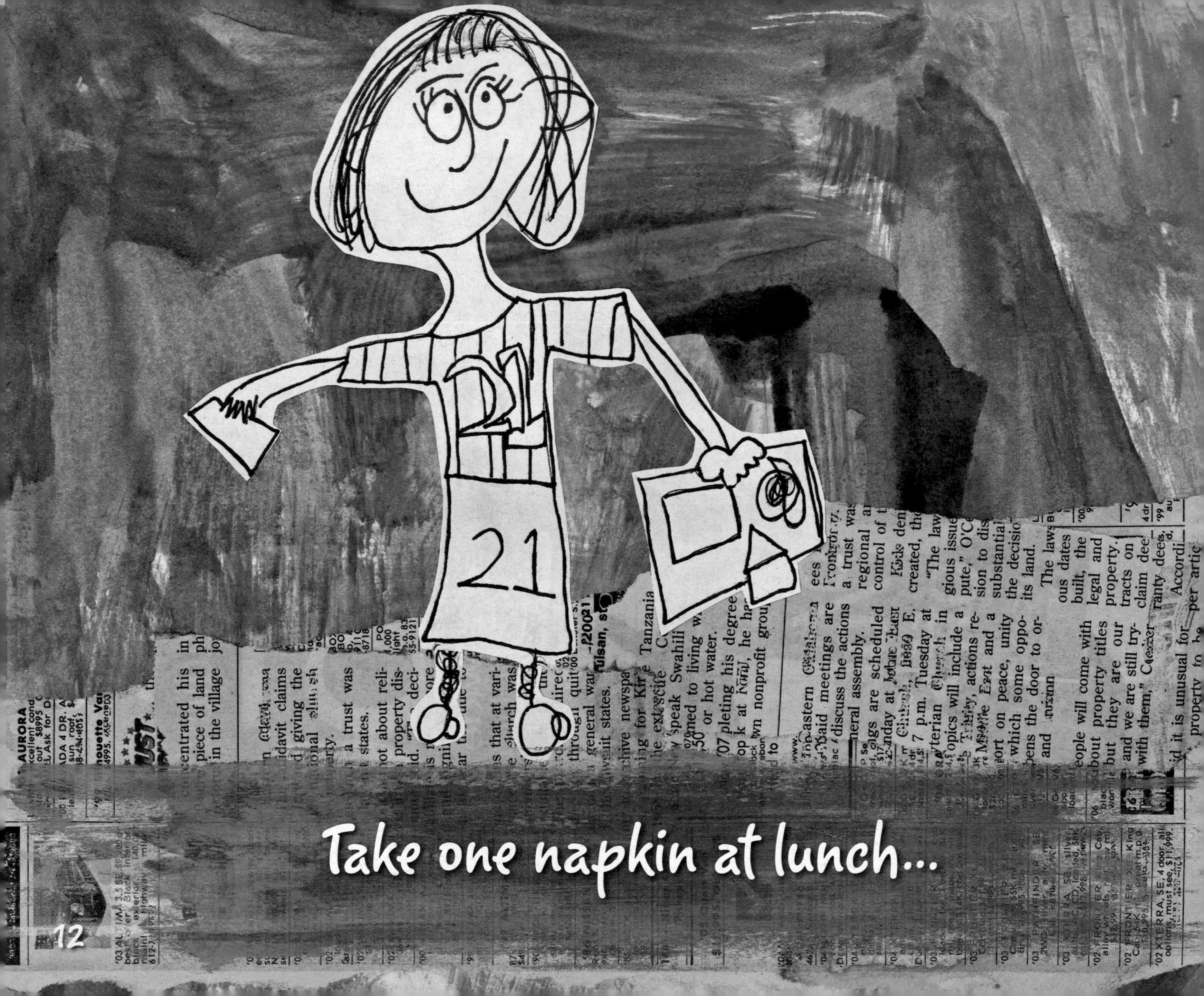

Take one napkin at lunch...

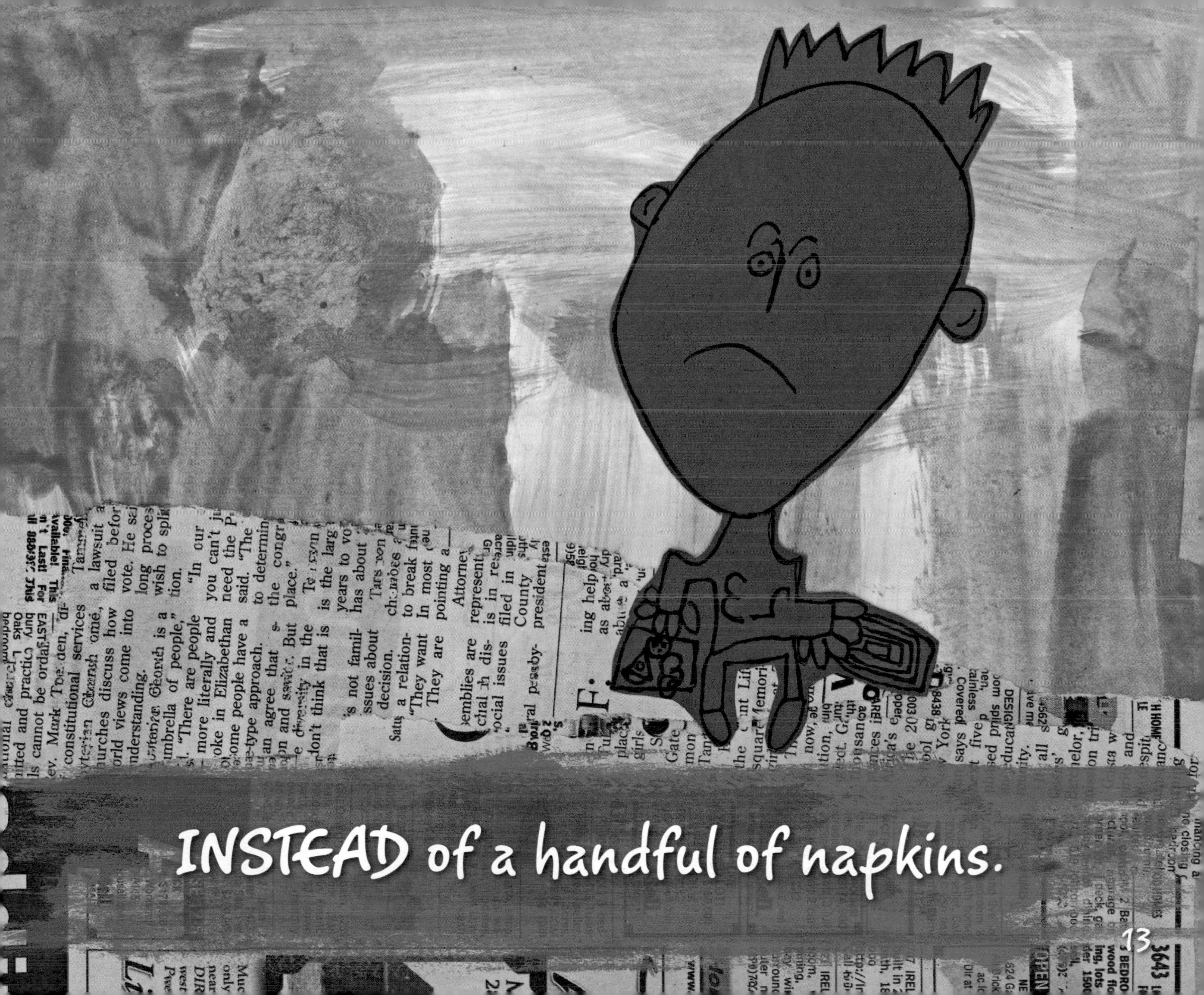

INSTEAD of a handful of napkins.

Keep our classroom doors closed...

INSTEAD of letting the cold air in.

Reuse old paper for
class lessons and projects...

INSTEAD of using new paper.

Turn the water off after we wash our hands...

INSTEAD of leaving the water running
while we dry our hands.

Help keep our playground clean...

INSTEAD of littering on the ground.

Recycle our trash...

Our class has learned how to make
the world a better place.

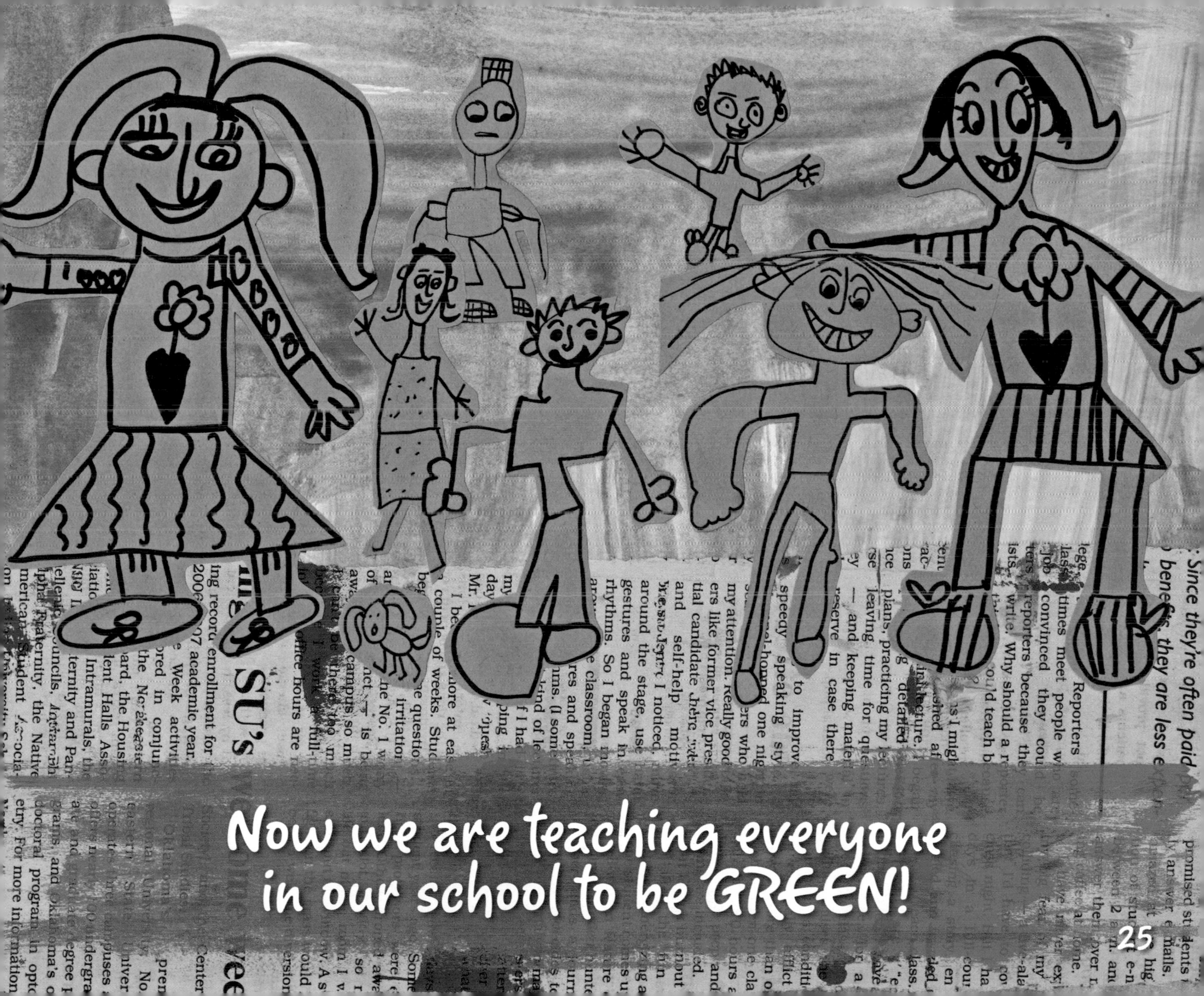

Now we are teaching everyone in our school to be GREEN!

Think of ways you can take care of our environment and GO GREEN!

1. _____

2. _____

3. _____

4. _____

5. _____

6. _____

7. _____

8. _____

9. _____

10. _____

11. _____

12. _____

13. _____

14. _____

This book was printed using recycled paper.
But do you know how recycled paper is made?

First, waste paper is collected and brought to a paper recycling plant. The paper is mixed with water in a huge machine that pulls the inks off the paper. Then, the clean paper-pulp mixture is put through screens that catch things like paper clips and staples. Usually, the clean pulp gets mixed with some new wood pulp so the paper will be stronger. Finally, the clean pulp is pressed into big sheets, dried, and put onto paper rolls.

Kids Are Authors®

Books written by children for children

The Kids Are Authors® Competition was established in 1986

to encourage children to read and to become involved in the creative process of writing.

Since then, thousands of children have written and illustrated books as participants in the

Kids Are Authors® Competition.

The winning books in the annual competition are published by Scholastic Inc. and are distributed by

Scholastic Book Fairs throughout the United States.

for more information:

Kids Are Authors® 1080 Greenwood Blvd. Lake Mary, FL 32746

Or visit our web site at: www.scholastic.com / kidsareauthors

Meet the Authors

Project Coordinators: Joyce Nickels, Erinn Rakes

Top row: Myla Rogers, A.J. Marler, JoHanna Caruthers, Trey Glover, Keagan Clemons, Michael Blower

Middle row: Keaton Tidwell, Reed Adams, Brody Tucker, Phoenix Bunker, Dominic Hadley, Desaray Crawford

Bottom row: Yadira Mares, Ethan Gilkey, Ariel Jimison, Trey Williams, Makaila Cox, Jaden Liston, Chaz Ostermeier

Our class is going GREEN!